THE

Aztecs

Sally Hewitt

Contents

Children's Press
A Division of Grolier Publishing
New York • London • Hong Kong • Sydney
Danbury, Connecticut

Who were the Aztecs?

About 500 years ago, Native American people called Aztecs lived in a country we now call Mexico. Legends tell how the Aztecs wandered for many years without a home. One day, their god, Huitzilopochtli, told them to build a city where they saw an eagle on a cactus. They saw this on an island in Lake Texcoco and there they built the great city of Tenochtitlán. For 200 years the Aztecs were rich and powerful.

An Aztec ruler was called the Tlatoani. The people were divided into classes. The noble class worked in the government. Common people were craftsmen, fishermen, and farmers. Rich people owned slaves.

Today, many Mexican people still speak the Aztec language. They also make pottery and weave cloth just as their Aztec ancestors did.

Moctezuma

Moctezuma was a rich and powerful Aztec ruler. He was carried around on a portable throne.

You will need:

Colored construction paper	Glue	Aluminum foil
Cardboard	Paints	Scissors
Ribbon and sequins		

Follow the steps . . .

1. Paint the outline of Moctezuma on his throne on the cardboard in bright colors.

2. Cut a feather headdress out of green paper and glue it to Moctezuma's head.

3. Glue on sequins and gold paper for his jewels. Decorate the throne with foil, ribbons, and gold paint.

Feather fan

Aztecs used the bright feathers of tropical birds to decorate shields and headdresses and to make fans.

You will need:

Cardboard tube   Colored paper   White paper

Gold cardboard   Glue   Gold ribbon

Adhesive tape

Follow the steps . . .

1. Fold strips of white, blue, and green paper. Draw half a feather shape on each strip. Cut them out.

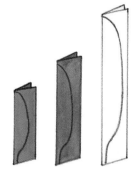

2. Snip the edges of the feathers. Paint the tips brown.

3. Cut this shape out of gold cardboard. Tape the feathers onto the back. Wrap the cardboard tube in red paper and decorate it with gold ribbon. Tape the fan to the inside of the tube.

Home and families

In an Aztec family, parents, grandparents, and children lived together in one house. When a baby was born a special ceremony was held. A tiny bow and arrow or tools were set out for a boy, and a spinning wheel and clothes for a girl.

Children from commoners' families worked
hard, and their parents were strict. When they
were old enough, girls helped in the home and
boys fished or worked in the fields. Boys and
girls went to separate schools. They learned
weaving, feather work, pottery, and other crafts.
Many boys trained to be warriors.

Coiled pots

Aztec potters did not use a potter's wheel. They made pots with coils of clay and smoothed them out by hand.

You will need:

Modeling clay	Modeling tool	Rolling pin
Paintbrush	Brown and black paint	Water

Follow the steps . . .

1. Roll out long strips of clay.

2. Make a base by coiling a strip in a circle. Coil more strips to build up the sides of the pot. Dampen the coils to stick them together.

3. Smooth out the coils with water and your modeling tool. Paint your pot with black and brown lines and simple shapes.

Picture writing

Speech

House

Motion

Wind

Aztecs made books called codices from bark or animal skin. They used picture symbols to tell stories.

You will need:

Long strip of white cardboard   Felt-tip pens

Follow the steps . . .

1. Fold the cardboard like this:

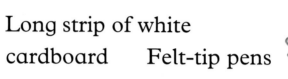

2. Make a list of Aztec picture symbols and add some of your own.

3. Write a story using the symbols. Ask your friends to use your list to help them read your story.

Water

Serpent

Dog

Grass

Alligator

Rain

Deer

Flower

Monkey

Rabbit

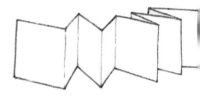
Deat
hea

Flint
knife

Eagle

Lizard

Gods and goddesses

The Aztecs believed that the gods controlled their lives and everything that happened in the world. To make sure the sun rose, the rain fell, and the crops grew, the Aztecs made sacrifices to the gods to keep them happy.

Tláloc was the god of rain.

Huitzilopochtli was the Aztecs' special god and god of the sun.

Coatlicue was the fierce goddess of the earth with a skirt of serpents.

They used prisoners of war as human sacrifices to the gods. They honored the gods with ceremonies at their great temples, as well as with singing, dancing, and feasts.

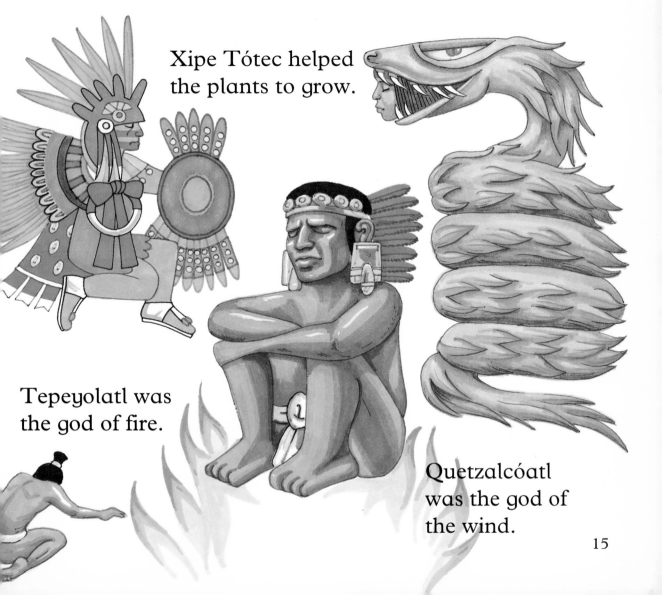

Xipe Tótec helped the plants to grow.

Tepeyolatl was the god of fire.

Quetzalcóatl was the god of the wind.

Pyramid

Temples were built on tall pyramids. Steps led
to the top where sacrifices and ceremonies took place.

You will need:

Yellow cardboard	Yellow paper	Small box
Ruler	Scissors	Pencil
Paints	Adhesive tape	Glue

Follow the steps . . .

1. Draw these shapes on the cardboard. Cut them out.

2. Tape the four pyramid sides together. Tape the square on top.

3. Wrap the box in yellow paper. Tape it on top of the pyramid.

4. Fold a strip of yellow cardboard to make the steps. Tape them on. Decorate your pyramid with paint.

Warfare

At the sound of the war drum, Aztec men left their homes and joined the army. Warriors wore stiff cotton suits and carried wooden shields. They fought with spears, bows and arrows, and fierce wooden clubs. The clubs were edged with sharp chips of volcanic rock called obsidian.

18

The Aztecs did not try to kill their enemies. Instead they took prisoners and sacrificed them to please the gods. A conquered city had to pay tribute to the Aztecs. Tribute was like a tax. It was paid with food, treasures, and useful materials. Tribute was used to feed the Aztec people and to give the nobles riches.

19

Eagle helmet

Aztec knights wore jaguar skins and feathered helmets into battle to give them the strength of wild animals.

You will need:

Brown paper   Orange cardboard   Pencil

Hole puncher   Brown paint   Glue

String   Scissors

Follow the steps . . .

1. Draw two beaks on the cardboard. Cut them out. Make sure they fit around your face.

2. Cut 16 strips of brown paper. Cut feather shapes along one edge. Glue them together so that they overlap. Glue them onto one beak. Paint some feather tips brown. Add eyes. Punch holes in the sides of the beaks. Thread string through the holes.

Aztec banner

Warriors in battle could recognize their commander by the colorful banner he wore strapped to his back.

You will need:

White and gold cardboard   Red paint
2 long cardboard tubes   Adhesive tape
Crepe paper (red and green)   Scissors

Follow the steps . . .

1. Copy these shapes on the white and gold cardboard and green crepe paper. Cut them out.

2. Tape the green crepe feathers to the back of the gold cardboard. Tape the other green shapes to the white cardboard. Paint on red stripes. Tape the cardboard tubes together and wrap with red crepe paper. Tape the other shapes to the tube.

INDEX

Entries in *italics* are activity pages.

© 1996 Watts Books, London,
New York, Sydney
All rights reserved. Printed in
Malaysia.
Published simultaneously in
Canada.
1 2 3 4 5 R 99 98 97 96 95 94

Editor: Annabel Martin
Consultant: Keith Lye
Design: Ruth Levy
Artwork: Cilla Eurich and
Ruth Levy
Photographs: Peter Millard

First American Edition © 1996 by Children's Press
A Division of Grolier Publishing
Sherman Turnpike
Danbury CT 06816

Hewitt, Sally.
    The Aztecs / Sally Hewitt
        p.   cm. -- (Footsteps in time)
    Summary: Describes the traditional way of life of the Aztecs.
Includes activities in which common items represent what the
Aztecs used, such as making a fan out of strips of colored paper
representing the feathers of tropical birds.
    ISBN 0-516-08071-7
    1. Aztecs--Social life and customs--Juvenile literature.
2. Aztecs--Material culture--Juvenile literature. 3. Creative
activities and seat work--Juvenile literature. [1. Aztecs--Social
life and customs. 2. Handicraft.] I. Title II. Series.
F1219.73.H48 1996   95-25252
972'.018--dc20   CIP AC